JUV
567.9
ALI   Aliki

         Digging up dino-
         saurs

DUE DATE			
MAY 3 0 1996	JUL 1 6 2002		
JUN 2 4 1996	JAN 2 5 2005		
JUL 2 3 1996	SEP 0 9 2005		
AUG 7 1996	OCT 0 5 2005		
AUG 1 2 1996	JUN 2 1 2007		
APR 1 4 1997	JUL 1 0 2007		
MAY 2 9 1997			
SEP.10.1997			
JUL 9 1998			
AUG 1 5 1998			

P9-CDA-891

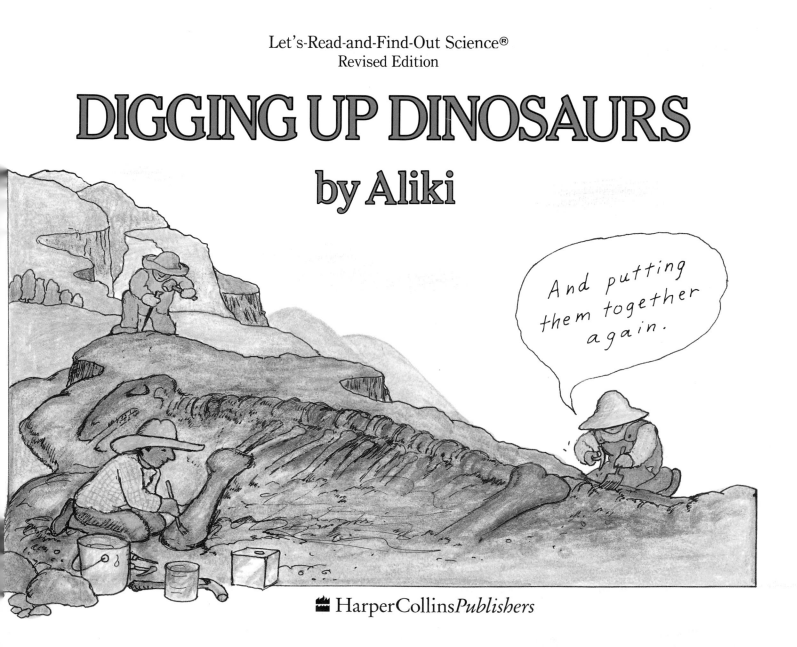

The *Let's-Read-and-Find-Out Science* book series was originated by Dr. Franklyn M. Branley, Astronomer Emeritus and former Chairman of the American Museum–Hayden Planetarium, and was formerly co-edited by him and Dr. Roma Gans, Professor Emeritus of Childhood Education, Teachers College, Columbia University. Text and illustrations for each book in the series are checked for accuracy by an expert in the relevant field. For a complete catalog of Let's-Read-and-Find-Out Science books, write to HarperCollins Children's Books, 10 East 53rd Street, New York, NY 10022.

Let's-Read-and-Find-Out Science is a registered trademark of HarperCollins Publishers.

Digging Up Dinosaurs

Copyright © 1981, 1988 by Aliki Brandenberg
All rights reserved. No part of this book may be used or reproduced in any manner whatsoever without written permission except in the case of brief quotations embodied in critical articles and reviews. Printed in the United States of America. For information address HarperCollins Children's Books, a division of HarperCollins Publishers, 10 East 53rd Street, New York, NY 10022.

Library of Congress Cataloging-in-Publication Data
Aliki.
  Digging up dinosaurs.
  (Let's-read-and-find-out science. Stage 2)
  Summary: Briefly introduces various types of dinosaurs whose skeletons and reconstructions are seen in museums and explains how scientists uncover, preserve, and study fossilized dinosaur bones.
  ISBN 0-690-04714-2.—ISBN 0-690-04716-9 (lib. bdg.)
  ISBN 0-06-445078-3 (pbk.)
  1. Dinosaurs—Juvenile literature. [1. Dinosaurs. 2. Fossils]
I. Title.
QE862.D5A34   1988   567.9′1   87-29949

Revised Edition

for Beverly Kobrin

DIGGING UP DINOSAURS

4

Have you ever seen dinosaur skeletons in a museum?

I have.

I visit them all the time.

I went again yesterday.

I saw APATOSAURUS.

stop that, you bully!

GRRR

EEE

Imagine putting it together!

Like a jigsaw puzzle.

Apatosaurus— once known as Brontosaurus.

I saw CORYTHOSAURUS.

I saw IGUANODON and TRICERATOPS.
I like to say their names.

SCOLOSAURUS was just where I had left it.

And TYRANNOSAURUS REX looked as fierce as ever.

TYRANNOSAURUS used to scare me.

I still can't believe how big it is.

Just its head is almost twice my size.

I'm not afraid of dinosaurs anymore.

Sometimes I call them "you bag of bones"
 under my breath.

I can spend hours looking at them.

I used to wonder where they came from
 and how they got into the museum.

But now I know.

I'm scared.

Here he is!

This is a little fella.

One swat of his tail would show you how little.

SCOLOSAURUS
(armored dinosaur)
plant eater

TYRANNOSAURUS REX
meat eater

Dinosaurs lived millions of years ago.
A few of them were as small as birds,
   but most were enormous.
Some dinosaurs ate plants.
Some dinosaurs ate the meat of other dinosaurs.
And some may even have eaten the eggs of other dinosaurs.

Dinosaurs lived almost everywhere on Earth.
They lived for millions of years.
Then they died out.
No one is sure why they became extinct.
But they did.
There hasn't been a dinosaur around for
   65 million years.

DIPLODOCUS

BRACHIOSAURUS

COMPSOGNATHUS

ORNITHOMIMUS

TYRANNOSAURUS

11

Until about 200 years ago, no one knew
  anything about dinosaurs.
Then people began finding things in rock.
They found large footprints.
They found huge, mysterious bones
  and strange teeth.
People were finding fossils.
They began asking questions about them.

Fossils are a kind of diary of the past.

They are the remains of plants and animals that died long ago.

Instead of rotting or crumbling away, the remains
were preserved, and slowly turned to stone.

1. 80 million years ago
Dinosaur dies and sinks into river.

2. Its flesh rots. Its skeleton is covered by mud.

3. In time, the mud and skeleton turn to stone.

4. Dinosaur is hidden for millions of years.

5. The Earth changes. Some of the stone breaks away.

6. 100 years ago
Part of the dinosaur is exposed.

Fossils tell about life on Earth long ago. Everything we know about dinosaurs comes from studying fossils.

Fossil hunters found more and more big bones
in different parts of the world.
Scientists studied the fossils.
They said the bones and teeth and footprints
all belonged to a group of giant reptiles
that lived on Earth for millions of years.
The giants were named DINOSAURIA, or terrible lizards.

1822

Mary Ann Mantell
found the first dinosaur
fossils, in England.
She discovered some
giant fossil teeth.

1825

Her husband, Dr. Gideon
Mantell, named the
animal IGUANODON,
or Iguana-Tooth.

Nine years later,
he found a mass of
IGUANODON bones.

1841

Dr. Richard Owen
named the giant
reptiles DINOSAURIA.

What finds these were!

People crowded into museums to see them.

But the dinosaur bones didn't just get up and walk there.

They had to be dug out of the ground, slowly and patiently.

Even today, digging up dinosaurs is not an easy job.
A team of experts must work together.

PALEONTOLOGIST
A scientist who studies ancient plants and animals.

GEOLOGIST
A scientist who can tell the age of rocks and fossils.

DRAFTSMAN
who draws pictures of the fossils.

WORKERS
who dig the fossil
out of the rock.

PHOTOGRAPHER
who takes pictures
of the find.

SPECIALISTS
who prepare the
fossil for the
museum.

This is how fossil hunters work.

First, they have to find a dinosaur.

They search along riverbanks and in quarries.

They climb up high cliffs and down into steep canyons.

With luck, someone spots a fossil bone
  poking through the rock.

The site is covered with a tent, and the work begins.

Sometimes the fossil is buried so deep, the rock
   around it has to be drilled or blasted.

Tons of rubble are carted away.

Scientists chip at the rock close to the fossil.

They brush away the grit.

They have to be very careful.

As soon as a bone is uncovered,
  it is brushed with shellac.
The shellac helps hold the bone together,
  so it won't crumble.
Then the bone is numbered.

Sometimes a skeleton has to be cut apart
  so that it can be moved.
The draftsman draws each bone in its
  exact position, and the photographer
  takes pictures.
That way, there can be no mix-up later,
  when someone tries to put the skeleton
  together.

When the bones are ready to be moved,
  they are carefully wrapped.
Small bones are wrapped in tissue paper
  and put into boxes or sacks.

Large bones are left half buried in the rock.
They will be dug out later, in the museum.
These fossils are covered with a plaster cast,
just as a broken leg is.

First, the parts of the fossil that show are covered with wet tissue paper, and then with strips of burlap dipped in wet plaster. Then the whole piece is wrapped in the same way. When the plaster dries, it becomes very hard. The tissue-paper covering makes the cast easier to remove later.

Each bone is then packed in straw, put into a crate,
and taken to the museum.

At the museum, scientists unwrap the fossil.

They finish digging it out of the rock.

They study the bone.

Scientists dig out the fossil in many different ways. They use a hammer and chisel, fine needles, power tools that work like a dentist's drill, special sandblasting machines, and even chemicals that dissolve the rock but do not harm the fossil.

They compare the bones to other dinosaur bones.

They compare them to the bones of other animals.

They try to figure out what size and shape the dinosaur was.

They try to find out how the dinosaur stood
and walked, and what it ate.

IGUANODON

First discovered and named by Dr. Gideon Mantell in England, 1825.

AGE: 115 million years ago
PERIOD: Lower Cretaceous
LENGTH: 9 meters (30 feet)
WEIGHT: 5,000 pounds
TYPE: Ornithischian (bird hip)
Herbivorous (plant eater)
Descended from Dinosaur CAMPTOSAURUS

This information has been gathered by studying many IGUANODON finds from all over the world.

Birdlike hip.

Rough skin. Exact color unknown.

Spiked thumbs used for digging and protection.

Hooflike bones show it sometimes walked on its front limbs.

Usually walked on two legs.

Tail used for balancing.

Here is its hip bone.

Horny beak used to tear up plants.

Thousands of flat teeth used to grind food. When the teeth wore out, they fell out and others grew in.

	Today	
Cenozoic	Quaternary	
	Tertiary	65
	Upper Cretaceous	
	Lower Cretaceous	136
Mesozoic	Upper Jurassic	
	Lower Jurassic	193
	Upper Triassic	
	Lower Triassic	225
	Permian	280
Paleozoic	Carboniferous	345
	Devonian	395
	Silurian	435
	Ordovician	500
	Cambrian	570
	Pre-Cambrian	
	Age of Earth	4600

AGE OF DINOSAURS

MILLIONS OF YEARS AGO

27

If there are enough bones, scientists are able
   to build a complete skeleton.
A frame is made in the shape of the dinosaur
   to support the bones.
The bones are wired together, one by one.
They are held in place with pieces of metal.
If any bones are missing, plastic or fiberglass ones
   are made to replace them.
You can hardly tell the new bones from the old ones.

After many months the work is complete.
The dinosaur skeleton looks just as it once did.

29

Until recently, only a few museums had dinosaurs.

Then scientists learned how to make copies of the skeletons.

The copy is hard to make.

It takes a long time.

The original skeleton has to be taken completely
    apart, bone by bone.

A mold is made for each bone.

The new pieces are made of fiberglass.

A fiberglass dinosaur is just as scary as the original,
    but much stronger and lighter.

The original bone is covered with rubber latex and an outer coating of fiberglass, to hold the rubber stiff. This is peeled off the bone to form the mold. The inside of the mold is brushed with resin and filled with fiberglass. Many dinosaurs can be made from the same molds.

Now museums all over the world have dinosaur skeletons.
And many people can spend hours looking at them,
the way I do.